W9-AXI-005

*What About
Homosexuality?*

YOUTH FORUM SERIES

A YOUTH FORUM BOOK

What About Homosexuality?

by Clinton R. Jones

THOMAS NELSON INC
Nashville and New York

Copyright © 1972 by Clinton R. Jones

All rights reserved under International and Pan-American Con-
ventions. Published in Nashville, Tennessee, by Thomas Nelson
Inc. and simultaneously in Don Mills, Ontario, by Thomas
Nelson & Sons (Canada) Limited.

ISBN: 0–8407–5320–9

Library of Congress Catalog Card Number: 70–39593

Printed in the United States of America

Dedication

To all of those counselees
who have broadened my vision,
deepened my understanding,
and given me a sense of
hope for the generations
which will follow.

Foreword

This book is one of a series in a unique publishing effort in which Youth Research Center, Inc., Minneapolis, Minnesota, has joined with Thomas Nelson Inc., Camden, New Jersey. The books are based on the very real concerns, problems, aspirations, searchings and goals of young people today as measured by the research center.

Central to the series is the belief that we all have a compelling need to turn to a core of faith for guidelines in coping with the world in which we live. Each book deals with a specific need or concern of young people viewed in relation to the Christian faith. By drawing upon the results of the surveys, each author is helped to speak more directly to the conflicts, values and beliefs of today's young people.

The significance of this series is enhanced, as well, by the scholarship and commitment of the authors. The grasp of the field in which each writes lends authority to their work and has established this series as a basic reference eagerly read and appreciated by young people.

Table of Contents

Preface

"What's it all about, Alfie?" is still being heard as one of the songs from a popular motion picture. Certainly the question, "What's it all about?", is asked many times by young people as they are maturing. It applies to many areas of life. Specifically to sex.

If researchers are correct in reporting that young men reach sexual maturity in their middle teens and that pregnancy is possible before the teens begin, then sex becomes important early in life. There always have been so many questions asked—or questions that come to mind but remain unasked because of timidity or fear—and so few answers provided.

Society generally has held the parents responsible for guiding, and instructing the child; however, we know that the area of sex has been too sensitive a subject for many parents to discuss. What parents do not teach, public and private schools are expected to teach. Here, too, until recently (this effort now is seriously threatened) too little has been taught, and usually too late for many young people. Let it be said, fairly and honestly, that the family, the school, and the church all have failed to help young people in this vital aspect of their maturing. Jesus asked, "What man is there of you, whom if his son ask bread, will he give him a stone?" (Matthew 7–9). There have been many requests for "bread," but too many "stones" in response.

This book is about a specific aspect of sexuality—homosexuality: the sexual response of one person toward another of the same sex. No words are more cutting, more condemnatory, more derogatory for the teenager than "faggot," "queer," "fairy," "pansy." To be labeled thus is devastating; the result may be social ostracism, even isolation. The usual response is to challenge such labels, true or not, by a denial, perhaps in the form of a threat ("Say that again and I'll knock your block off!"), or even a fight. It is a myth that femininity in the male and masculinity in the female and homosexuality are one and the same; yet, because of that myth, many young people are falsely labeled by their friends, even their families, and the result is considerable anguish.

Perhaps the injustices many young people have suffered have prompted my own particular concern and my desire to help whenever possible. In my thirty-year ministry, I have concentrated on teaching, counseling, and working with teenagers; I also have served as a college chaplain and as a military chaplain, and this background gives me a base from which to speak. Keeping pace with each generation has not been easy over the years, and I may not always have learned all the "in" words, phrases, or even attitudes; however, quite consistent through the years has been the need for enlightenment in the realm of human sexuality.

Fortunately, and I say, "praise be!", attitudes now are changing. As recently as five years ago, the publishers of this series of books might not have ventured to include this volume; but now there seems some break in a sky which has been dark and cloudy for so long. It is my hope that my present effort may let in just a little more light.

Clinton R. Jones

1. What About Sexuality?

What about homosexuality? Perhaps we can't deal with such a topic unless we think first about sexuality. Frankly, no one ever will honestly understand homosexuality until he sees it in the full setting of man's total sexual need and response. It is amazing that for centuries man has been expanding his knowledge with ever increasing acceleration, especially in science; yet it has been only within this century and, really, only within the past decade or two that responsible students have taken a serious interest in man as a sexual being. Now, at long last, some extremely helpful reports are being released, and considerable more research is in progress.

One of the great mysteries of life is still unanswered, and it always may be so: this is the question of why we have the sexual feelings we have. In other words, why are some men attracted to women, some to other men, and some to both men and women? There is no absolute answer. Anthropologists, psychologists, sociologists, geneticists, and other scientists have been searching for an answer for years, but the question remains unanswered. Of course there have been and there are many theories, but in the last analysis we still must regard them as theories only, and not the final truth. John Money *, associate professor of medical psychology and pediatrics at Johns Hopkins University's School of Medicine, and one of the world's leading authorities on the subject of sexual identity, is of the opinion that no one knows the etiology of any sexuality, except that it is not genetic. However, I am confident that this point may be challenged.

One of the most significant studies of sexuality, of course, was undertaken at Indiana University in the early 1940's under the direction of Dr. Alfred Kinsey, an anthropologist, and his coworkers. An extensive study was made of five to six thousand men, and his report, *Sexual Behavior in the Human Male*, was released in 1948. It was a shocker! With one fell swoop many long-held myths about man's sexual nature and experience were exploded. In particular, readers were stunned by the statistics indicating the prevalence of homosexuality. The researchers concluded that 4 percent of the men studied seemed to be totally homosexual, meaning that the total sexual drive of four of every one hundred men is projected toward his own sex. This was a far higher figure than expected.

* *Sex Errors of the Body*, John Money. Baltimore: Johns Hopkins Press, 1968. *Transsexualism and Sex Reassignment*, Richard Green and John Money (ed.). Baltimore: Johns Hopkins Press, 1969.

However, the next statistic was the real surprise: 37 percent of those studied admitted that they had had a homosexual experience to the point of orgasm at some time in their lives. Beyond this, the study also revealed a considerable number of men who, although never involved in a physical homosexual act, had a desire to do so. In my own counseling I have talked with men who fall into this last category—some to the extent that they may be committed homosexual persons who for several reasons never have been physically involved.

With this last group included, the Kinsey report would seem to indicate that about half of the men studied either had been sexually involved with another man or was at least interested in such an involvement—a conclusion that other researchers feel is much too strong. The results of a later study of women indicated that, for the categories listed above, the figures can be reduced to about half.

We must realize, however, that Kinsey was *not* working with a random sample of the general population at the time he conducted his surveys. Thus, translating his findings in terms of the general population really cannot be done. His contribution *does* indicate that myth and fact often are unrelated, one to the other.

Briefly, then, what does this research tell us? Merely that the incidence of homosexual behavior is much greater than we might suspect, and that it touches perhaps half of the total male population of the country. This is an important point to keep in mind when one realizes how isolated, how frightened, how strange a young person may feel if he thinks he has homosexual feelings, or has such an encounter with another of the same sex. I once counseled a young man who had grown up in a city of about forty thousand people. As he grew up and sensed his homosexuality, he was absolutely sure there wasn't another person who had similar feelings in the entire city. Such fear hardly helps develop a strong, healthy self-image.

It is apparent from the statistics that a large percentage of the population has both homosexual and heterosexual tendencies. Although the word "bisexual" has been used in the past to describe this kind of person, the term "ambisexual" now is being used to describe the person who can and will respond to both sexes. Obviously this varies with each person. As we all know, each person is distinctly an individual; no two persons are exactly alike, and therefore there will be great variety in the area of sexual need and fulfillment. There will be those who, although primarily heterosexual, have homosexual inclinations and those who, although considered to be primarily homosexual, function adequately with persons of the opposite sex, and may even develop strong emotional feelings about them. These persons, of course, have a difficult time sorting themselves out. In counseling more than five hundred persons who have indicated concern over homosexual feelings, I found that perhaps a third or more were married or were involved, at least, in a deep relationship with a person of the opposite sex.

At this point I should say something about the word "homosexual." I realize that it is primarily used as a noun, but I feel that this is a mistake because I believe that we should stop using labels. We are trying to do this with other minority groups. We hope that barriers, long too old and long too high—barriers erected because of skin color, religious persuasion, ethnic origin, even sexual identity, will break down. We sense that the less labeling we do, the greater the hope for a society that will work in unity toward common goals to save rather than to destroy the world.

Secondly, I believe that the word "homosexual" should be used as an adjective to describe a kind of feeling or a type of sexual response. "Heterosexual" is also an adjective, for it implies the desire for a physical act involving someone of the opposite sex. In other words, we should not refer to a person as "a" homosexual. He or she has homosexual desires, is involved in a homosexual relationship, or engages in certain homosexual acts. I presume that the word could be used as an adverb if we referred to someone as "acting homosexually."

In my mind, to use the word "homosexual" as a noun boxes a person in, and as a counselor, I have worked with those who would even erroneously label themselves. They would begin the first interview by declaring, "I am a homosexual." But as the counseling progressed, new insights would develop and other feelings would surface, so that eventually he would discover heterosexual desires and needs strong enough so that heterosexual marriage became possible.

I fear it will be a struggle to win this word battle. Even those involved in the homophile movement find it too easy to use the word "homosexual" as a noun. However, I still believe that the principle is valid. Acceptance of the homosexual person will be greatly helped if we will stop categorizing and accept the fact that there are persons with strong homosexual feelings, and others with dominant or exclusive heterosexual feelings.

Before I proceed too far, I would like to discuss some thoughts about the word "sexual." I am convinced that this word is so broad, so encompassing, that when it is used, speaker and listener often are not communicating. The English word, "love," is used to describe too many kinds of feelings, whereas in Greek, for example, there are several words which we translate as "love," but which have specific applications.

Webster's *New World Dictionary* defines the word "sexual" as "characteristic of or affecting sex." Although sex has played a significant role throughout the centuries, it was not until the twentieth century, and particularly through the contribution of Sigmund Freud, that man became truly aware of how deeply his sexual feelings, needs and responses reach into almost every aspect of his life. The truth now seems to have become fact: Man is a sexual being and much of his motivation, many of his decisions, and a considerable part of his conduct rest upon his sexuality.

As Dr. Mary Calderone of SIECUS * has stated, every person is a sexual person; even priests or nuns who have accepted the vows of chastity still remain sexual persons.

* Sex Information and Education Council of the U. S., 1855 Broadway, New York, N. Y., Mary S. Calderone, M.D., M.P.H., executive director, has compiled *Sexuality and Man*, Charles Scribner's Sons, New York, publisher.

They have opted for continence, but this does not take away their sexuality. Psychologists and other students of human behavior tell us that the human being becomes a sexual person early in life; babies seem to find pleasure in contact with sexual organs, and both men and women remain sexual into the final years of a long life.

All this being true, how are we going to deal with the word "sexual"? Must it be limited to just the physical or, more specifically, to the genital? I do not think so. When we use the word "sexual" we should think of it at three different levels: the emotional, the sensual, and the genital, or physical. I should like to expand on these three:

The Emotional. Who does not admit to emotional reactions to other persons which can be analyzed only as strong, positive responses about being with that person? You may go to a restaurant and be served by a waiter or waitress, and you feel comfortable about this person. You enjoy the way you are greeted and how you are served; there may be some conversation, as well, which goes beyond the mere business of eating a meal. When you return to the restaurant, you may hope to be served by the same person; you may even ask for his or her table. This kind of experience happens all through life, touching every area of our human involvement—the playmates we chose, the teachers we liked, the aunt or uncle who was special, or the best friend in high school.

We have not considered these feelings as sexual. But Freud and those who have followed him, even those who have modified many of his concepts, tell us that sex lies at the bottom of such responses. We do realize that when we move into deep emotional relationships, sexual feelings are evident. Frequently, intense, long sustained, deeply meaningful emotional relationships exist without either sensual or physical involvement. Is not the story of the Russian composer, Tschaikowsky, a case in point? His love was, in part, directed toward his patroness, Madame Von Meck, with whom he never exchanged a word and whom he saw only twice and in fleeting fashion. There was nothing sensual about the relationship, yet it was emotionally real enough to be considered part of his total sexual response. What I am eager to say is that the emotional can and does live by itself without the sensual or the physical.

The Sensual: This word refers to that which involves our senses: touch, sight, sound, smell, and taste. This is another level of our sexuality. Each of these five senses contributes to what is pleasurable, comforting, exciting, even arousing. Although we generally associate the sensual with the emotional or the genital, there are indications that this, too, can exist by itself. The need to touch, the feeling of being close to another human being, the desire to express sensuality can be satisfied through contacts which really are neither emotional nor genital.

I have counseled many young people with strong homosexual tendencies who said that they have met and been attracted by someone and that, after the exchange of only a few words, have gone to bed together, but without genital contact or orgasm. Just holding each other and falling asleep was all that seemed necessary, and each separated in the morning with a sense of satisfaction. Certainly in boy-girl relationships there are instances where two people meet only once. They may have sensual contact which is surely a real part of their sexual need, but no genital contact and no emotional attachment.

The Genital: It is at this level that we usually have used the word "sexual"; however, as I have said, this is too limited. "Genital" means that the sex organs are involved. I presume it is difficult to separate the genital from the sensual, since the physical is involved in both instances. However, there are situations in which genital sex is involved without true sensual enjoyment or emotional response. The men who frequent railroad stations, for instance, seeking genital satisfaction but without even knowing their partners, or the men who seek out prostitutes receive just physical satisfaction and no more.

I am not trying to say that these three levels of sexuality very often exist separately; perhaps they seldom do. Usually they exist in combination and, of course, in the responsible, committed relationship of two loving persons, the three levels are bound together. In a good marriage, husband and wife should know, appreciate, and delight in a full sexuality which is emotional, sensual, and genital.

But since this book is dealing with homosexuality, I would like to end this first chapter by indicating that homosexual persons, as well as the rest of society, would do well to think of homosexual response in terms of these levels. Too often, when the word "homosexual" is used, the focus is on physical acts which are considered perverse, deviant or just plain unmentionable. In all fairness, the emotional and the sensual levels should be emphasized, too. Both literature and history are filled with accounts of men and women, often highly honored, who have had deep emotional commitments to those of their own sex and we know, too, that often the sensual was involved, too. What their physical relationship may have been has not always been known, but perhaps, in the final analysis, this last level is not that important in terms of human love, of human understanding, of human concern, and of human compassion.

My conclusion, therefore, is that one cannot have an adequate or honest understanding of homosexuality without placing it against the broad backdrop of human sexuality.

2. What About Cure?

"Can you help me?" That often is one of the first questions a high school boy asks me in his first interview. Such a conference is usually traumatic—so difficult for the boy and none too easy for the counselor who sees that the boy is nervous, tense, uncomfortable, even frightened; he hardly knows what to say or how to describe what may be in his mind and heart.

He has come to talk about his homosexual feelings. Perhaps this is the first time he ever has talked to anyone about his private, personal, sexual attitudes and responses. Since he may be revealing what, to him, is the very center of his life, he naturally is desperately fearful about what damage, what harm his counselor might cause him. The boy is in pain, and it is pain which has brought him to the counselor's office—the pain of knowing or fearing he has homosexual feelings.

There are as many different situations as there are different people, but there also are some fairly typical experiences. There is the boy who, although he never has had any physical contact with another male, has developed a "crush" on a boy or a young man. They may have some communication, or it may be simple hero worship; or perhaps he actually has become physically involved with one or several boys. He has responded to his homosexual experience, and now harbours great fear and guilt about it. Or he may have formed a close, intimate relationship with an older man— a family friend, or a teacher—and although the relationship has been helpful and satisfying, he is troubled as to where it is leading him. These are just a few examples of the many situations faced by such young men.

Knowing all-too-well society's condemnation of homosexuality, this boy is afraid that his future may be one of rejection, of thwarted relationships, of untold unhappiness. He may be desperate. Fortunately, he has come for help; some who have not have become so depressed that they have committed suicide.

His is a call for help. What does this really mean? In the beginning, no doubt, his appeal is for change. He really would like to feel differently about his sexuality. He does not like, does not want his homosexual feelings. I presume that anyone in pain goes to the doctor hoping that the pain is minor, and that it will disappear with one visit, one prescription. It is distressing to learn that the cause of the pain may be deep-seated, may not respond to any known therapy or may even indicate a condition which cannot at this time be cured. The best the physician can promise is every available help to alleviate the pain as much as possible.

Where do we begin with this boy? First of all, I believe, he must be helped to deal wth guilt about his homosexual feelings. He needs some of the thoughts outlined in the previous chapter explained to him, particularly concerning the development of sexuality and underscoring the point that no one knows with certainty why we possess the sexual tendencies which we have. We know there are theories, such as psychological repression before three years of age, or an unfortunate emotional development during the oedipal period (four to six years of age) when there is evidence of the close, binding intimate mother and the hostile father. There is the theory that our sex is learned in the pre-puberty period between the ages of six and 10 or 12, through our play experience or other personal contacts during these years. And there are those who maintain that there is a genetic, glandular, or physical cause.

When all is said and done, these still are theories, and the fact remains that we just don't know how, when, and why homosexual feelings develop. The one point of general agreement seems to be that our sexual tendencies have been developed, basically, by at least the age of puberty. What we consciously know about them, how they will unfold themselves, and how much they will vary is part of the mystery of life. The one honest, helpful response we can give this boy is to let him realize that, as far as we now know, he didn't consciously bring about, out of his own desire and will, the sexual feelings he now has.

Even after he has learned this so that his sense of responsibility for his sexuality and some of his guilt feelings have been reduced, the question, "But can you cure me?" will still be foremost in his mind. Here, of course, is the knotty problem. Here, too, the battle lines are drawn. What is this "war" all about?

The early sex researchers, Havelock Ellis *, Krafft-Ebing **, Hirschfield *** and others seemed to take the position that the homosexual person was an "invert." In other words, he was in such a fixed position that little could be done to make a real shift in his sexual preferences. No detailed therapies aimed at "cure" were developed. Freud, too, had to face up to the homosexual condition of some of his patients. Although he believed psychoanalysis was helpful in so many areas of human personality difficulty, he held out little hope for truly changing homosexual tendencies or desires. His famous "Letter to an American Mother" spells this out:

> "I gather from your letter that your son is a homosexual. I am most impressed by the fact that you do not mention this term yourself in your information about him. May I question you, why do you avoid it? Homosexuality is assuredly no advantage, but it is nothing

* Henry Havelock Ellis (1859–1939). *Sexual Inversion.* (Part IV, Vol. 1 of *Studies in the Psychology of Sex.* New York: Random House, 1936, page 361.

** Richard von Krafft-Ebing (1840–1902). *Psychopathic Sexualis.* New York: Putnam, 1965, pages 245–383 and 469–500.

*** Magnus Hirshfield (1868–1935). *Sexual Anomolies.* Norman Haire (ed.). London: Encyclopaedic Press, 1952, chapters 11–15.

to be ashamed of, no vice, no degradation, it cannot be classified as an illness: we consider it to be a variation of the sexual function produced by a certain arrest of sexual development. Many highly respectable individuals of ancient and modern times have been homosexuals, several of the greatest among them (Plato, Michelangelo, Leonardo da Vinci, etc.). It is a great injustice to persecute homosexuality as a crime and cruelty too. By asking me if I can help, you mean, I suppose if I can abolish homosexuality and make normal heterosexuality take its place. The answer is, in a general way, we cannot promise to achieve it. In a certain number of cases we succeed in developing the blighted germs of heterosexual tendencies which are present in every homosexual, in the majority of cases it is no more possible." *

However, regardless of this letter, many of Freud's followers and others known as the neo-Freudians, as well as experts belonging to other schools of psychiatry, believe sexual proclivity can be changed or at least can be adapted so as to make an adequate, satisfying heterosexual adjustment possible. In the past two decades many analysts and therapists have indicated success—to list a few: Irving Bieber, Albert Ellis, Daniel Cappon, Charles Socarides, Lawrence Hatterer.** More recently the behavioral scien-

* "Letter to an American Mother." *American Journal of Psychiatry,* CVII, April, 1951, page 787.
** See Bibliography, page 84.

tists have developed techniques called "aversion therapy" *
and "aesthetic realism." ** Each passing year we receive
reports from therapists that a new approach is meeting with
success.

It is important to point out that in almost all instances
there are some specific conditions which must exist. First
is the strong, dominant desire of the young person for
change; in other words, this must be someone who is in considerable pain about his homosexuality and wishes to live
and to function heterosexually. The second is the person's
age, and this is significant. There is some consensus that for
successful therapy, the patient should be in his teens or
early twenties. Trying to change the confirmed homosexual
person who is past 30 is difficult. A third condition is the
willingness to give the therapist ample time. In some cases,
both individual and group therapy may take as much as 350
hours, although some reports indicate a shorter time span.
Fourth, financial resources must be available. Few therapists can work without fees, and unfortunately there are

---

* "Behaviorists began to try curing people of phobias and alcoholism,
most commonly with 'aversion therapy' in which electric shock and
nauseating drugs such as apomorphine were used to make patients associate their problem behavior with displeasure. During the following decades
behaviorists went on to attack addiction, smoking, stuttering, sexual de-
viations and finally all of the disorders of the psychiatric clinic." *Sexuality
and Homosexuality*, Arno Karlen. New York: W. W. Norton Co., page
588.

** *The H Persuasion*, Sheldon Krantz (ed.). New York: Definition
Press, 1971. The Study of Aesthetic Realism with Eli Siegel: "Aesthetic
Realism sees homosexuality as a phase of the tendency for love of another
person to become simply a form of loving oneself—which tendency has
been a cause of despair in man." Page 47. (Reprinted by permission of
the publishers.)

not many clinics where there are no fees or at least minimal ones. This, of course, means that hundreds, often thousands of dollars, must be committed.

What comments can be made about such help? There are those who line up on the other battle front and hold that such efforts are ridiculous, a waste of a person's time and money, and do not prove anything. The arguments are many:

(1) Even if such therapies are helpful, there just aren't enough qualified therapists to even begin to cope with the problem. Considering the fact that there are apparently millions of persons in the United States who can be identified as having almost total homosexual response as well as a significant larger population who have been involved in physical homosexual situations at some time in their lives, it may be fair to question whether or not there is an adequate supply of therapists to effect change of sexual identification or feeling should such be desired. Therapists who believe change is possible do indicate that there must be some committment in terms of both time and fees. Where are qualified therapists, the clinics, the money?

(2) Is there adequate evidence that these therapies are successful? Has there been sufficient time to test the results? Have consistent follow-ups proved that those "cured" remained "cured" or was there a return, at least in some cases, to previous behavior?

(3) How satisfied, how fulfilled, have these "cured" patients really become? This, I fear, is a question which would be extremely difficult to answer.

(4) The most important question of all, perhaps, is this:

Were such "cures" really necessary anyway? The question asked by many therapists and also by many involved in the expanding homophile movement is this: "What is so terrible about a homosexual way of life? Can it not be fulfilling? Are there not millions who make an adequate adjustment to this life style? Wouldn't it be better if, instead of attempting a "cure," our energies were expended toward education, social action, and civil rights; toward changing the attitudes of society so that the homosexual does not have to experience the pain society thrusts upon him?

Now we should go back to the young man who is sitting in the office and asking, "Can you help me?" As his question makes us see the pain he is in, it also reveals the predicament of the counselor or therapist. How often we would like to say, "Just a minute, I have a few sugar-coated pills here in my desk drawer and if you take three a day for a week, all of your homosexual feelings will disappear and you'll be all set." It would all be so simple.

Any counselor, of course, needs to know the limits of his abilities. I am a pastoral counselor with a thirty-year ministry of working with people. Over the past few years I have been meeting regularly with some persons on a sustained basis for weeks, months, even years. Modestly I admit to a certain knowledge of homosexuality, coupled with some expertise in working with homosexual persons, both individually and in groups. I have read extensively, completed many courses in various aspects of both theoretical and clinical psychology, studied sexual ethics. I have completed a thesis on the subject of counseling the homosexual person and yet I would never tell such a person I could or even would attempt to "cure" him.

Should he be eager to proceed with a therapeutic technique which might help him reach his goal of a "cure," I would do all I could to refer him to the proper resources. It would be fair to explain, as I already have noted, that considerable time and money might be involved.

At this juncture, I would like to think about the word "cure." It obviously implies sickness, crippling, disease. The physical body, as we all know, must be cured when it gets sick. Man's mind, we say, also becomes sick; the patient is depressed, alcoholic, addicted, has delusions, is schizophrenic, can become dangerous to others, even drives himself to suicide. He needs help and care. Fortunately, we have many able psychiatrists, psychologists, social workers, and counselors of varying skills and disciplines who are attempting, often with great success, to cure these troubled persons. Even in the realm of sex, therapists such as Masters and Johnson * are trying to rectify sexual malfunctioning and to make unhealthy, unhappy situations healthy, again, and happy and satisfying for those involved. It is when we raise the question of whether the person with homosexual tendencies is "sick" that we find ourselves in the center of the battle. On one side we find the researchers and therapists who have developed "cures;" on the other side is a significant number of researchers and therapists who re-

---

* W. H. Masters and V. E. Johnson, *Human Sexual Response.* Boston: Little, Brown, 1966. Masters and Johnson, *Human Sexual Inadequacy.* Boston: Little, Brown, 1970.

spond differently. Wainwright Churchill, Martin Hoffman, Evelyn Hocker, Judd Marmor * are among those who maintain that the homosexual person is not "sick" merely because of his homosexuality. This is not saying that some homosexual persons do not exhibit evidence of deep-seated neuroses, of serious anxieties, of deep depression, even of psychoses; but it is saying that many homosexual persons function with as much success and satisfaction as do heterosexual persons.

It has been natural for many counselors and therapists to conclude that homosexual persons are sick because those who come for help have been in distress. Because the majority of homosexual persons are not known in society, it has not been easy to evaluate their state of mind, their emotional stability, nor the success of their relationships or vocational achievements. Today as more and more people feel freer to admit their homosexual identity, particularly through the organizations which make up the homophile movement, it is apparent that an untold number of responsible, productive, well-adjusted homosexual persons can be found in every walk of life: lawyers, psychiatrists, teachers, social workers, clergy, businessmen, carpenters, bricklayers, artists, writers, physicians—the list could go on and on. Homosexuality seems to appear at every vocational, cultural, and social level. Some homosexual persons may be wealthy, others poor; often they are talented, often they are limited; many reach their life goals, many do not. Conclusion: There is the possibility, then, that the homosexual

* See Bibliography.

person is not very different from the heterosexual person except that he or she has sexual interest in or preference for a person of the same sex.

Once again we return to the young man with the question, "Can you help me?", meaning, "Can you cure me?" If by "cure" he means being rid of homosexual feelings or desires, those of us eager to help will be seriously frustrated. After we honestly give him the option of seeking another therapist who may (and I must say "may" because "cure" is not always possible) provide the results he desires, and he still wishes to continue counseling, what can we offer? I believe there are ways in which we can help:

(1) If he is in his middle teens, we can make it clear that, since he still is maturing emotionally and sexually, it is too early for him or perhaps for anyone else to know what his true sexual identity may be. There is some evidence which indicates a person may not know his true identity until his mid-twenties. Whatever sexual tendencies were established early in life, his recognition or full evaluation of them may not be possible until he has matured in other aspects of his life.

(2) We can help him understand that many persons have a mixture of homosexual and heterosexual feelings. As life unfolds, he will be discovering through various relationships where his greatest emotional and sexual satisfactions may be.

(3) We can deal directly with his guilt feelings if he expresses them. He may not need to feel as guilty as he does.

(4) We can let him know that he is not alone. Refer-

ences to the homophile movement will tell him that those who are admitting their homosexuality are also involved in securing acceptance and civil rights for other homosexual persons.

(5) We can assure him that researchers and others in the helping professions are trying to understand and to help the homosexual person, as well as attempting to translate to society, as a whole, the meaning of homosexuality.

(6) We can let him know that we are there to listen to anything he wants to tell us about his sexual feelings, fantasies, or activities. This means, of course, that we be prepared to accept, without censure, whatever he says.

What kind of "cure" can we offer? If he says he wants to be "straight," he may need referral to other therapists. If "cure" means relief of pain, or reducing it to a tolerable level, some of the alternatives outlined above may prove helpful. There is no question that as each young person begins to face up to whatever homosexual feelings he may sense, he or she needs the opportunity to find acceptance, understanding, and counsel. The past has badly failed this person; let us of the present do all we can to help, even to holding out the possibility that the future may bring greater hope.

3. What About the Family?

"Does your family know?" is often a question I ask a young person who has come to discuss his homosexual feelings. In almost every instance the answer is "No!", usually followed immediately with, "And I don't want them to know, either!" It is not difficult to understand why he would not want to reveal homosexual desires or activities to parents or others in the family. This is not just a characteristic of young people. By far the greatest proportion of the homosexual persons I have counseled have never wanted to discuss their sexual life with their families.

Obviously, some families know. They almost always know, of course, if their son or daughter has been involved in a situation which caused trouble at school, with the law, or with the parents of another young person with whom he or she may have had a sexual encounter. Also, parents are apt to find literature or letters which arouse their suspicions. Rarely, two young people are discovered in a compromising situation. All too often parents, particularly mothers, sense much more than the boy or girl imagines.

What are some of the reasons a homosexual person may hesitate to tell his family? Perhaps first is his fear of censure and rejection. No one enjoys being rejected. We all want acceptance; we want to know that our families are happy with us, proud of us. Although young people today are being freed from many prejudices of previous generations, they are thoroughly conscious of the cultural lag between ages, and the varied attitudes on racial, religious, and social problems. This is particularly true of sex. Views differ on the so-called sexual revolution. Some experts believe that none has taken place; others believe we are at its height; a few say the revolution is over, that we simply need to come to terms with it. Revolution or not, we must face the reality of a sharp shift in the sexual attitudes of youth today in contrast to their parents.

As I sense the social climate regarding homosexuality, I must admit that the average young person who gathers the courage to discuss homosexual feelings with his family may need preparation for a traumatic experience. Obviously this is a general statement, for there may be some enlightened parents who could deal with the situation humanely and adequately.

A young person who risks discussing his homosexuality with a family member probably will not be totally rejected, will not be told, "There is the door—out you go!" More to be feared is creation of an attitude that would seem suddenly to set him apart. Immediately everyone is on guard.

Suspicions arise in many directions. If he is a young man, there may be questions about his friends, and are they also "queer?" Where does he go at night? What does he do? Will he get into trouble? Will his homosexuality affect his chances of future happiness and success?

The perceptive young person also may hesitate to talk to his family about homosexual feelings because he fears he may arouse guilt feelings, particularly in his parents. This is a reasonable fear. Over and over again parents ask themselves, "Where did we go wrong? How could this have happened? We must have failed somewhere." A young person usually is not prepared to cope with such a response.

What can be said to help parents deal with their own sense of guilt or failure? Certainly they should know that opinion is divided, even among experts, as to what causes homosexuality. Some experts working in the field of human sexual response seem convinced that sexual feelings are developed early in life. The Freudian theory about the oedipal period indicates that during these years a boy forms a strong emotional attachment to his mother, while a girl's strong attachment is to her father. Freud believed, therefore, that it was important that a child grow out of this stage and into a good relationship with the same sex parent.

Some psychiatrists proclaim that if a boy's mother makes him the basic object of her love so that she is over-possessive and over-protective, she may keep him from establishing a good relationship with his father. The result, according to this theory, is that the seeds for a later homosexual response may be planted. On the other hand, if the father, during this oedipal period, rejects his son, is hostile toward him, and feels threatened because the mother gives the child all her attention, he may detach himself from his son to the extent that he contributes directly to the son's homosexuality. The same relationship, in reverse, applies to the female child, with homosexual tendencies the theoretical result.

What about this fairly prevalent theory? Again let me restate that we are dealing with theory, not fact. Case histories of certain homosexual persons seem to substantiate this theory; however, many committed homosexuals do not fit this framework at all. In my own counseling I have known both men and boys who had had unusually fine relationships with their fathers and did not feel a close, binding, intimate relationship with their mothers. And college counselors have told me of working with young men and encountering many instances in which the mothers' influence was far too dominant, while the father relationship hardly existed at all; yet the students exhibited heterosexual and not homosexual feelings.

I find it tragic that parents should be stricken with guilt because a son or a daughter seems to have homosexual tendencies. I can understand their grief, but even if they were in some way unwittingly responsible, it is futile to worry about what is past. It is impossible to go back and change something. The significant question parents now must ask themselves is this: "How shall we react? What must our attitudes be?" I would like to list some suggestions I hope will be helpful:

(1) Understand. Love might seem a better word than understand; however, although the homosexual person needs, wants, hopes for love from his parents, his great

desire is for understanding. The phrase, "I will love you in spite of what you are," is not helpful. The homosexual person did not just sit down one day and say, "I think I'll be homosexual." His feelings have been surfacing little by little over a long period of time. There have been the difficult, painful, anguishing moments of feeling alone, strange, alienated, and sinful because of his sexual responses and acts. Surely it is difficult and painful enough for him to try to understand and cope with his own emotions, which can be overwhelming at times; and so there is the hope and the need that others, especially those who should be closest to him, will understand, or at least make the supreme effort to understand. Parents who know little about homosexuality can find books to read, and knowledgeable, responsible people from whom they may learn through discussion.

(2) Accept. Understanding is one level, acceptance another. Often we say, "I understand why you do what you do, but I cannot accept what you do." This expresses a common attitude toward homosexuality, as well. There are those who will say to the homosexual, "Indeed, I not only understand that it is not your fault that you have homosexual feelings but I also understand that you have a right to express your homosexuality physically; however, please do not ask me to accept what you do."

I have heard many pastors make statements in this vein: "Of course I can understand the homosexual person, but I certainly cannot condone or accept homosexual physical acts." Would we say to the heterosexual person, "I understand your heterosexuality, but I cannot accept how you express it sexually"? If we say we understand the homosexual person, we must, if we are going to accept him, too, move on to accept whatever the expression of his sexuality might be.

(3) Respect. Leaders in the homophile movement feel that the most important goal is to help the homosexual person attain self-respect. For too long he has felt like a second-class citizen, and there is justification for this feeling, since this has been society's attitude. In my counseling, I find homosexual persons who are deeply depressed. They feel unworthy, unlovable, unclean. If I can do nothing else, I try to help them toward a better image of themselves. Here, then, is where the family can play a significant role. When they know one of their own is homosexual, they at least can hold him in respect—the same respect by which other family members are held. The homosexual son or daughter does not have to be apologized for nor, above all, condemned. He has as much right to respect as any other family member.

(4) Protect. What a person confides to his family is one thing; what he wishes outsiders to know may be very different. I consider protection important because I have known of unhappy situations where a family failed to keep the confidences that were intended for them only. Parents have been guilty of spreading information around to aunts, uncles, cousins, neighbors, and so on. This is a flagrant breach of confidence. Merely revealing homosexual feelings to any family is enough of a trauma without the family broadcasting the information. This is a private matter, and the family should respect it.

(5) Counsel. Therapy means care. All good relationships

should be therapeutic. Although we cannot choose our family, we do know that family relationships open up many channels to help, understanding, solace, and support. The family can offer the best possible therapy in times of need and stress. However, the family must know some of the basic counseling rules: to listen without being shocked, to avoid being condemnatory, to let persons make their own decisions, to be prepared to offer advice if it is sought. The young homosexual person needs to talk out feelings, as do heterosexual sons or daughters, but too often the one with homosexual feelings is neither heard nor helped.

It also may be the family's responsibility to at least find out if the young person wants professional help. Coercion, however, should be avoided. Too often parents rush their son off to a doctor, a pastor, or a psychiatrist. This usually creates considerable embarrassment for him, and builds up such resistance that, although these professionals could have been helpful, therapy is made impossible. I have known cases where a son or daughter has been dragged from one counselor to another, all because the parents did not get the satisfaction *they* wanted. The therapist may have suggested that the young person did not need professional help, but the parents, not accepting this fact, still relentlessly sought a counselor who would do what they wanted. Such attempts create great anger in the young person, with the result that the parents are shut out and further offers of help rejected.

Instead, parents could say something like this: "John, we realize your situation is not easy. Considering society's attitude toward homosexuality, as well as the many difficulties in establishing personal relationships, perhaps you would like to share some of your thoughts and feelings with someone outside the family, a professional person who understands more of what is involved than we do. If you wish, we will try to find the right person to help you." This kind of overture is itself therapy and may bring an accepting response.

Having discussed how a family can help itself face a homosexual situation, I return to the statement I made at the beginning of this chapter: the average homosexual is not known as such by his family, does not want to have to cope with his family in this regard, and even though there may be suspicion, prefers to avoid any confrontation. The family may also choose to leave many thoughts unspoken.

Let us face the fact that perhaps 90 percent of all homosexual persons are not identifiable to others. After all, what are the distinguishing characteristics of the homosexual person? The male is supposed to be effeminate, with a slight, delicate body, limp wrist, high-pitched voice, possibly even a lisp. The female is thought to be masculine in appearance with short hair, and a deep voice. She wears dungarees and no make-up. A few of these types are known in the homosexual world, but they may not necessarily maintain a homosexual life-style. Freud's theory, again, was that the most masculine of men possess some femininity, and the most feminine of women some masculinity, with the mixture of the two varying from person to person. All of us know men who exhibit strong feminine qualities, both physically and emotionally, but who have satisfactory heterosexual relationships. The same also applies to the woman with dominant masculine characteristics.

Millions of homosexual men and women are part of the nation's social structure without their homosexuality being known to family or many close friends. The teller at the bank, the man who pumps gas, the church school teacher, the salesgirl at the cosmetic counter, the hospital intern, the plumber, the stock broker—any one of these persons whom you meet over and over again may possess strong homosexual drives, may even be involved in a long-term homosexual relationship, yet this is not indicated by the way they dress, or walk, or speak, or act.

As a homophile leader commented at a recent national conference: "If every homosexual person turned green overnight, the whole society would be thrown into such a state of shock, it would not know how to cope." A clergyman nearing retirement once said to me, "But I really never knew a homosexual." My response was, "I suspect you have known hundreds in your life—you just didn't recognize them."

I will write later on about the homophile movement in this country, but one of their slogans is, "Out of the closets and into the streets." They are trying to convince homosexual persons that they should "take off their masks" and become identifiable. It may be true that many homosexual persons, especially students and other young people belonging to predominantly youth-centered groups, are heeding this challenge but by far the largest group of homosexual men and women will remain quietly hidden. For them the risks of identification still are too great. Until society in general adopts more open, more accepting attitudes toward homosexuality, I suspect that "the closets" will remain full.

4. What About the Church?

Change is essential for every person, every institution. Practicing as I do a counseling ministry, I repeat over and over again that if I did not believe people could change, I would find another way to spend my life. With gratitude I acknowledge that I know alcoholics who have ceased using alcohol, addicts who have forsaken the use of drugs, men who have become more faithful to their marriage vows, women who have matured into better mothers, and students who progressed from academic failure to dean's list status.

Jesus of Nazareth believed in change. His ministry was dedicated to change: to help the deaf hear, the blind see, the crippled walk, the sinner begin a new life. Also he felt called to reinterpret many of the social and religious customs of his own heritage. Did he not heal on the Sabbath day? Did he not forgive those who were considered unforgivable? Did he not associate with publicans and harlots? He was never willing to settle for the status quo. The demand he felt was to do "the will of The Father who hath sent me" (John 5:30), and this seemed to move him into many areas of controversy to such an extent that the traditionalists, the conservatives conspired to nail him to the cross.

I believe that Jesus expects his church to change. If we believe that Jesus is timeless, that his Gospel is for all ages, then I believe, also, that his message must be made relevant for each generation. There were moments during the last decade when it seemed as if he would not be able to speak to youth but now, with the appearance of "the Jesus Cult," "Jesus Rock," and "Jesus Folk Opera," it seems that he is being known and heard. Truly, indeed, although such forms are a departure from the traditional, his basic "Good News" is still proclaimed.

We do not know all of Jesus' feelings about sex. The Gospel narratives provide little help. He did emphasize time and again that we should love one another. He stressed the value of human ties through his own relationships with Mary Magdalene, Lazarus, Peter, Mary and Martha, and, of course, the beloved John. Forgiveness was available to all, even to a woman who had committed adultery. He upheld the institution of marriage as it was known in his time, and he even brought to it a new dimension—a man was an adulterer, just as was a woman, if there had been sexual unfaithfulness. If Jesus were to comment directly on today's sexual values and behavior, would he side with the conservatives or the liberals? Is it fair to suggest that, at the very least, he would be against any kind of prejudice, but particularly that which sets race against race, nation against nation, even Christian against Christian?

The church is thought of as Christ's body, yet it is doubtful that the church has always acted as Jesus might have wished—particularly during such periods in history as the Spanish Inquisition when so-called heretics were burned at the stake, or when churchmen owned other men in slavery, or when the church failed to speak out as five million Jews were being destroyed by a European madman. The church, then, in spite of what it is called to be, does not always fulfill its true mission. It must continue to move toward being better, and it must always be ready for change. A living body continually undergoes change and renewal; so, I believe, must the body of Christ if it is to be recognized as a living, not a dead church.

While we may not know what Jesus' attitude toward sex in our day might be, we do know the stance of today's Christian churches. At the same time, we are beginning to see changes in the attitudes of Christian leaders and in their conventions where denominational judicatories reshape precepts, constitutions, by-laws, and canons. Changes include church stands on pre-marital sex, birth control, and abortion, but we will limit our discussion here to homosexuality.

First, what has been the attitude of the church throughout the centuries concerning man's sexual relationships with other men? Some reference must be made to the ancient Jews and to the Old Testament. Such sexual conduct was not approved. Many reasons are obvious. First of all, a man needed a large family, particularly several sons. This was his and his family's security. Who was admired more than Jacob who had twelve sons? The early Jews were agrarians—first shepherds, then possessors of Canaan, the land of "milk and honey." Human labor was needed. Infant deaths were frequent and the length of life considerably shorter. A men's sexual energy had to be used for the primary purpose of begetting children. Any diversion of this sexual drive would have to be thought of as perversion.

The story of Sodom and its destruction by fire illustrates the apprehensions felt about "men lying with men." Scholars now tell us that the original tale of Sodom did not concern sex; rather, the sin of Sodom's citizens was their failure to provide proper hospitality to strangers—indeed a serious breach within that social culture. It was later biblical interpreters who attached a sexual connotation to the story, but the fact that they did so indicates that they were eager to impress upon their people how truly abominable such sexual acts were considered by God.*

Jesus made no direct comments about homosexuality. This does lead one to the possible conclusion that if he had thought it was the terrible sin those before him had felt it to be, or those who followed him have believed it to be, he would have spoken out against it. Certainly he didn't hesitate to speak out openly, frankly, about other acts or attitudes he knew were against the will of God. As noted earlier, he does comment on marriage and on adultery. Again, in his own time, the family was the integral unit of

* See *Homosexuality and the Western Christian Tradition*, D. S. Bailey. London: Longmans Green & Co., 1955.

society; Jesus would not wish to see it shaken. Still, it would seem that he did not feel that establishing a family was the only way to find purpose in life or fulfill a certain destiny. To our knowledge, he himself did not marry. More than this, he established a social unit which was a radical departure from the accepted family structure. Did he not say to those whom he called to follow him that they were to forsake all family ties? There was to be no established "home." "The foxes have holes and the birds of the air have nests, but the Son of Man hath no where to lay his head" (Matthew 8:20). We cannot be sure how many of his twelve disciples were married. Apparently Peter was married since there is a reference to his "mother-in-law," but for lack of any other evidence it would seem that the others may have been single.

Many scholars and writers have speculated about Jesus' own sexuality. What fair comment can be made? The traditional Christian creeds emphasize that he is "God of Gods," yet "very man," "incarnate"—born of human flesh. The nature of Christ, then, is true God, true man. For centuries within the history of the Christian church, Jesus' "humanness" has been minimized, but there is no justification for this. The Gospels reveal a human Jesus who expressed the emotions of other human beings: joy, sorrow, pain, anger, love. There are tender accounts of his personal relationships. When his great friend, Lazarus, died, Jesus wept (John 11:35); when Jesus apparently needed the comfort of a home, he found Mary and Martha in Bethany, one to share his thoughts, the other to provide food for his body. Twelve men shared his life for three years. What could his relationship have been to Mary Magdalene? Apparently it was close. John, the son of Zebedee, is referred to as the "beloved disciple," with the Scriptures indicating Jesus' closeness to him. John was one of the first to be chosen; he was with Jesus on the Mount of Transfiguration; John was "lying on his breast" (John 13:25) at the Last Supper, and he was the one disciple to stand at the cross until the bitter end.

If Jesus was the perfect human being he always has been thought to be, he must have known sexual feelings. Over and over the Bible tells us that sex in itself is good, that it is God-given, God-intended as the means through which we come into close relationships with others. Why, then, should Jesus have been denied sexuality? How he responded to his sexual feelings always will remain conjecture; however, I wonder if Jesus did not respond emotionally and sensually to other persons.

The Epistles provide a few comments on homosexuality. Although to me not as condemnatory as the church has interpreted them to be through the centuries, still they certainly are not permissive. We must remember, however, that the Epistles were written during the last half of the first century and the early years of the second century A.D. Paul is the primary architect or author of the Epistles. Paul can be considered an ascetic. Even the basically healthy attitude of the ancient Jews toward sex finds no place in Paul's writings, and the human qualities of Jesus, with his love for persons is minimized.

This is perhaps understandable when we think about Paul's own personality, his heritage and the historic setting of his life. Although born a Jew, he was a product of Hellenistic dualism which greatly stressed the spiritual and deprecated the physical. According to this philosophy, which originated with the Greeks, those things belonging to "the spirit" were deemed highly virtuous, while those qualities associated with "the physical" were discredited. In his early writings, Paul was so convinced that the second coming of Jesus was immediately at hand when "the new Kingdom" would be proclaimed, that he suggested men not even marry—although rather grudgingly, it seems to me, he stated, "It is better to marry than to burn" (1 Corinthians 7:9). His reasoning seems to have been that since a whole new world of relationships was imminent, there was little point in establishing further human commitments in this world.

Today some theologians lament the direction in which Paul and the neo-Hellenists pointed the church; in fact, they will go so far as to state that such an emphasis distorted the Gospel of Jesus so that we may have lost much of the true meaning of all that God intended in the Incarnation.

Perhaps it would be helpful to look again at the early years of the Christian church. The writers of the Epistles were living in the midst of a pagan, sensual Roman world. Every kind of sexual license was known. Cities such as Corinth were "pleasure centers" where everything physical was emphasized. Such a life was hardly consistent with the Gospel of Jesus which, although it did not deny the physical, the pleasurable, the joyous, it did attempt to place "the things of this world" in perspective with "the treasures of heaven."

Jesus did not call *all* men to give up their possessions. Apparently he did not want to destroy marriage or family or home. He seemed to understand the need for human relationships. He was known to his enemies as a "worldly" man who did not hesitate to eat with the rich or associate with tax collectors, prostitutes, and others who were identified with things physical and material. However, throughout the Gospels we see Jesus helping people establish a kind of balance for their lives. While dining with Zacchaeus, a man who was hated for his riches and his selfishness, Jesus did not ask him to give up all that he had; instead, he challenged him to sell half of what he owned and give to the poor, for in this way he would not only find social acceptance but also a new self-respect. Jesus seems to have wanted to keep the physical and the spiritual in balance.

If Jesus himself had gone to Corinth, he might have had some of the same feeling that Paul had; however, my belief is that he might have dealt differently with the situation. Paul, in his anger about the conduct of the people and with his concern for de-emphasizing the physical, and his belief that the second coming of Christ was at hand, felt compelled to speak as he did. For Paul, it would seem, any kind of sexuality did not fit into his scheme of things, particularly sexual acts which were only for pleasure and not for producing children. However, it does not seem apparent that he felt homosexuality was worse than other sexual responses.

We must remember, also, that in the medieval church, which was basically characterized by monasticism, mysticism, celibacy, and asceticism, we see again the strong emphasis on Pauline theology at war with paganism. "The World, *the Flesh*, and the Devil" emerged as the arch enemies of Christ and his church. Submerged was the humanity of Jesus and the human warmth of the Gospels. Forgotten, too, was the natural humanity and sexuality to be found in the pages of the Old Testament.

William Temple, former archbishop of Canterbury and one of the most provocative theologians of modern times, noted that Christianity is actually one of the most materialistic religions in the World because it rests on two cardinal doctrines: God made man and God was made man.* God in his wisdom created man, the crown of his creation, out of the dust of the earth and endowed him with human flesh. The Garden of Eden can be regarded as a paradise of joy and pleasure. Secondly, in his eagerness to make himself fully known to man, God became human flesh and dwelt among us. Flesh was dignified enough for God to assume it, but this thought seems to have been lost as the church moved through the centuries; flesh became evil, the enemy of Christ, and the abode of the Devil. No wonder some Christians felt they must flagellate it, starve it, deny it, burn it and, above all, keep it from being the natural, sexual body which God intended it to be.

This medieval spirit not only has pervaded the church and its law, but has influenced the course of secular law so

* Quoted in *Sex in Christianity and Psychoanalysis* by William C. Cole. New York: Oxford University Press, 1955, page 8.

strongly that it remains with us today. In fact, it lives within the minds of many who call themselves Christians, and within the precepts governing many Christian churches today. The seventeenth century Puritans were imbued with it and labored diligently to see that the customs and the laws of the new world reflected their religious beliefs. It wasn't until the present century that the challenge came.

And now the church is facing change. It may have begun at the end of the last century when theologians, mostly Protestant by tradition, rediscovered Jesus the man, and began to expound the so-called social Gospel. Biblical scholars asked the church and the world to see, to know and to appreciate Jesus as the human being he was. A renewed, warm humanity emerged from the New Testament so that preachers, teachers, and writers began to proclaim "the real Jesus."

What part this has played in today's sexual revolution may be questionable. Perhaps the church's influence has been minimal. Many always have considered it basically reactionary in spirit, but I contend that it played some part in changing the sexual attitudes—a change with which we must now deal. Sorting out the causes of any revolution is none too easy; suffice it to say that there always are many flowing streams which eventually converge to create the broad, fast-moving rivers which may overflow the dams intended to provide control. The majority of social scientists indicate that the work of the early sex researchers, the writings of Freud, the publications of the Indiana Sex Institute, the new sexual freedom stressed by such popular therapists and authors as Albert Ellis and, more recently, Hugh

Heffner with his *"Playboy Magazine* philosophy"* all have been forces behind America's changing sexual attitudes and habits. There have been Christian leaders, too, who with a new interpretation of the Gospel have been attempting to provide a code of Christian ethics which would challenge many rigid precepts and restricting laws of the church.

The phrase "situation ethics" creates great consternation in the minds of some Christians, great hope in others. The basic argument is that any particular situation may have to be dealt with individually, that one cannot have rigid rules since there always must be exceptions. Examples: a city sets speed limits; however, ambulances and other emergency vehicles may need to break these established laws. Or, a person does not break into another man's home, but if he sees smoke coming from it, he might break in to be sure those inside are safe. Or, although speaking the truth is considered a virtue, we might, in a certain situation, lie about the whereabouts of a person to someone seeking to harm him.

There is some evidence that Jesus was a "situationist." He healed on the Sabbath, drove the money-changers out of the temple, and stopped men from fulfilling the law by stoning a woman to death. All were acts in which he met a situation by challenging or breaking the law.

Among those who ascribe to situation ethics are Christian leaders who are convinced that the church must rethink its attitudes toward birth control, abortion, divorce, premarital sex, homosexuality, and other aspects of family life and sexuality. They are challenging the church to reinterpret, to re-evaluate, and to change rigid and restricting positions.

New attitudes toward homosexuality are being shaped. This varies from church to church, but the attitudes and possible changes in the major churches are summarized here:

The Roman Catholic Church: The long-held position has been that homosexuality did not place one in any state of sin. The only problem faced by Roman Catholics is that physical homosexual acts are not allowed. This seems to be a firm and official position. However, I have heard many Roman Catholic priests state openly that if a penitent, in confession, is absolutely convinced that any act he has committed is not sinful, then it need not be confessed. This is a matter of individual conscience. How many Roman Catholics feel comfortable within this framework, I do not know.

The Dutch Catechism, although perhaps not in great favor with the Vatican, does provide a relaxed attitude:

"There are a certain number of people whose eroticism cannot be directed to the other sex, but apparently only to the sex to which they themselves belong. Lack of frank discussion has allowed a number of opinions to be formed about them which are unjust when applied generally, because those who have such inclinations in fact are often hard-working and honorable people.

"It is not the fault of the individual if he or she is not attracted to the other sex. The causes of homosexuality are unknown. In their human isolation, they look for friendship. But even where they find true and loyal responses, the perfect fulfillment of their human

longings is not granted them. Ultimately all homosexual (or rather, homo-erotic) tendencies come up
against the discovery that the sexual in men can only
find its natural fulfillment—as may be deduced from
human structure—in the other sex. Those who know
that they are homosexual should discuss the matter
with a doctor, a spiritual director, or someone prudent
and competent. They must also try to learn that
greatness of life consists of giving and receiving.

"The very sharp strictures of Scriptures on homosexual practices (Genesis 19; Romans 1) must be read
in their context. Their aim is not to pillory the fact
that some people experience this perversion inculpably.
They denounce homosexuality which had become the
prevalent fashion and had spread to many who were
really quite capable of normal sexual sentiments." *

Now a few American Catholic theologians are speaking
out with some boldness. In his recent book, *Sex: The Radical View of a Catholic Theologian,* Michael Valente writes
that "the prohibition against homosexuality stemmed from
the traditional belief that sex was necessarily and intrin-
sically procreation-oriented. Persons suffering from this
socially unaccepted difficulty should be made to realize
that their relationships can be good, especially if love is
present. They should be encouraged to seek relationships
that are meaningful and constructive, and that can contribute to the development of their personality as loving." **

* *A New Catechism: Catholic Faith for Adults.* New York: Herder and
Herder, 1969. Part IV, page 384.
** *Sex: The Radical View of a Catholic Theologian,* Michael Valente.
New York: Bruce, 1970.

The Greek Orthodox Church: This has been a basically conservative, traditional body within Christendom. To my knowledge, Orthodox theologians and leaders have not addressed themselves seriously to this subject. I believe that their position on homosexuality is similar to the official position of the Roman Catholic Church.

The Episcopal Church: No official position ever has been taken except that the church's 1967 General Convention passed a resolution asking that serious consideration be given to studying the topic, along with other matters touching on human sexuality and Christian family life. A study of attitudes toward homosexuality, *The Homosexual Problem—Theirs and Ours,** was released three years later. This was the result of a questionnaire sent to bishops, priests, laymen, laywomen, and seminarians. One expected result was the disclosure that the bishops were the most conservative and the seminarians the most liberal on all issues involved.

This report concluded that, "with regard to the homosexual, any effort by the church ought to be twofold:

(1) Helping people to recognize that, as long as homosexual activity is carried out between consenting adults, the persons involved may be acting as 'normally' as anyone else in society.

(2) Seeking ways to combat stigmatizing and discriminatory practices (police surveillance, vocational prejudice, armed forces discharge, etc.), such as those mentioned in the report and those brought to light by other investigators."

* Published by Seabury Press, New York.

Among Protestant churches, of course, there is a great variety of opinion. The British Society of Friends stated in its 1963 report, *Toward A Quaker View of Sex*, that homosexual acts were not in and of themselves immoral.

A quote from this particular text reads, "Further we see no reason why the physical nature of a sexual act should be the criterion by which the question whether or not it is moral should be decided. An act which expresses true affection between two individuals and gives pleasure to them both does not seem to us to be sinful by reason alone of the fact that it is homosexual. The same criteria seem to us to apply whether a relationship is heterosexual or homosexual." *

The Unitarian Universalist Association, at its General Assembly on July 4, 1970, adopted the following statement:

"Recognizing that:

1. A significant minority in this country is either homosexual or bisexual in their feelings and/or behavior;
2. Homosexuality has been the target of severe discrimination by society and in particular by the police and other arms of government;
3. A growing number of authorities on the subject now see homosexuality as an inevitable sociological phenomenon and not as a mental illness;
4. There are Unitarian Universalists, clergy and laity, who are homosexuals or bisexuals;

* Friends Home Service Committee, London.

THEREFORE BE IT RESOLVED: That the 1970 General Assembly of the Unitarian Universalist Association:

1. Urges all people immediately to bring an end to all discrimination against homosexuals, homosexuality, bisexuals and bisexuality, with specific immediate attention to the following issues:

   a. Private consensual behavior between persons over the age of consent shall be the business only of those persons and not subject to legal regulation.

   b. A person's sexual orientation or practice shall not be a factor in the granting or renewing of Federal security clearance, visas, and the granting of citizenship or employment or term of employment in armed services.

2. Calls upon the UUA and its member churches, fellowships, and organizations immediately to end all discrimination against homosexuals in employment practices, expending special effort to assist homosexuals to find employment in our midst consistent with their abilities and desires.

3. Urges all churches and fellowships, in keeping with our changing social patterns, to initiate meaningful programs of sex education aimed at providing a more open and healthier understanding of sexuality in all parts of the United States and Canada, and with the particular aim to end all discrimination against homosexuals and bisexuals."

The United Church of Christ, through its Council for Christian Social Action approved on April 12, 1969, this resolution:

> "Whereas homosexual practices between consenting adults in private endanger none of the properly protective functions of civil law, and
>
> Whereas laws against consentual homosexual practices between adults in private violate the right of privacy and are virtually unenforceable, except through the abhorrent practices of police entrapment and enticement, and
>
> Whereas such laws have no effect on the degree of homosexuality (as indicated by various studies abroad showing that homosexuality exists to no greater extent in countries without such laws than in the United States), and
>
> Whereas present laws and government practices regarding employment and military service of homosexuals are based on false assumptions about the nature of homosexuality in general and the danger of homosexuals to society in particular,
>
> Therefore the Council for Christian Social Action hereby declares its opposition to all laws which make private homosexual relations between consenting adults a crime and thus urges their repeal.
>
> The CCSA also expreses its opposition to the total exclusion of homosexuals from public employment and from enlistment and induction into the armed

forces, especially the dismisal of less than honorable discharges from the armed forces for homosexual practices with consenting adults in private. The CCSA supports dismissal of homosexuals from public employment and from the armed forces and their prosecution under the law when they have been found guilty of homosexual practices in public, against children and minors, or where force is used.

The CCSA also opposes, where they exist, police practices of entrapment and enticement in their attempts to enforce laws against homosexual practices and solicitation.

Finally, the CCSA encourages the UCC Conferences, Associations, and local churches to hold seminars, consultations, conferences, etc., for honest and open discussion of the nature of homosexuality in our society."

The Lutheran Church in America voted on July 2, 1971, at its Biennial Convention in Minneapolis that:

"Scientific research has not been able to provide conclusive evidence regarding the causes of homosexuality. Nevertheless, homosexuality is viewed biblically as a departure from the heterosexual structure of God's creation. Persons who engage in homosexual behavior are sinners only as are all other persons—alienated from God and neighbor. However, they are often the special and undeserving victims of prejudice and discrimination in law, law enforcement, cultural mores and congregational life. In relation to this area of concern, the sexual behavior of freely consenting adults in private is not an appropriate subject for legislation or police action. It is essential to see such persons as entitled to justice and understanding in church and community."

Many inter-denominational Christian bodies have been concerned with homosexuality. The Council on Religion and the Homosexual was founded in San Francisco and now has chapters in several states. Local councils of churches have established study and social action groups leading, occasionally, to organization of homophile groups, information centers, and counseling services. There have been other efforts, such as that of the George W. Henry Foundation of New York, chartered in 1947 and backed primarily by a board of clergy, which has served effectively in the areas of education and counseling.

Finally, some comment needs to be made about the emergence of what are known as "Gay Churches" or "Gay Christian Congregations." These are made up primarily of homosexual persons who have felt rejected by the established churches. Often they are led by pastors who openly identify themselves as being homosexual. Particular mention should be made of The Universal Fellowship of Metropolitan Community Churches, headquartered in Los Angeles, with missions in other California centers and several other states; The American Association of Religious Crusaders in Nashville, and The Church of the Beloved

Disciple, a liturgical church serving many hundreds in New York. These congregations are not eager to form separate churches, but they feel that until the established churches are able to accept the homosexual person, until he feels comfortable in their midst, and until he is given opportunities to contribute leadership, then it may be necessary for "Gay Churches" to continue their existence and perhaps to expand.

Will the church face the challenge of change in its attitude toward homosexuality? It does seem that it is beginning to do so. Let us hope that it will continue to re-examine and reshape its traditional positions. The future should hold many interesting developments.

5. Other Questions

I don't really know who is reading this book. A writer never does. However, my intention has been to write primarily for teen-age and college-age young people. Because of their own homosexual feelings some of my readers may be looking for specific, personal help. Others may simply be eager for more information about this particular sexual identity in order to help themselves develop their own attitude toward people they know now, or expect to meet. This chapter is intended to help both groups by dealing with specific topics.

WHAT ABOUT THE LAW? In this country, significant changes are taking place. Books have traced the treatment by society, through the ages, of those convicted of homosexual acts. At some periods in history homosexual acts were punishable by burning at the stake, by hanging, and by torture. Long prison sentences have been endured, as well as heavy fines, confiscation of property, and even banishment from community or country. The laws on the books in most of our states still are punitive and restrictive. In some instances, there may be imprisonment for thirty years.

Historically, one of the first permissive laws regarding homosexuality was contained in the famed Code Napoleon enacted in France in 1810. Gradually, other European countries began to relax their laws. However, it was not until 1954—almost 150 years later—that the British Parliament created the Wolfenden Committee to study homosexuality and prostitution. This committee, supported by the Church of England and other Christian denominations, produced a careful study which resulted in actual changes in the law.

These revised laws removed from the list of criminal offences those sexual acts which are not an affront to public decency, do not involve coercion or duress, and are not engaged in by any person under the age of 21. Although this law covers both sexes, it really affected men only, since homosexual acts on the part of women were not considered an offense. Basically, this same law now has been enacted in Canada.

Most European countries now have laws similar to Great Britain's although the age of consent varies. In some countries it is 21; in others—Denmark, for example—it is 18. The Netherlands has reduced the age of consent to 16. Germany and Austria recently have adopted consenting laws. Apparently Russia still holds to a rigid, restricting code.

In the United States, Illinois was the first state to follow the English changes. The Model Penal Code proposed by the American Law Institute has recommended change, but states have been slow in writing their recommendations into law. However, as revisions begin to occur, penalties for homosexual acts are being deleted. Connecticut's new liberalized law became effective on October 1, 1971. Oregon, Colorado, Alaska, and Idaho are adopting changes and, in some instances, the age of consent will be 16; in others, 18.

As I note the lowering of the voting age I see the increasing number of marriages in which one or both is under 21 and when young men can enlist in the armed forces at 17, as well be as drafted for battlefront duty while still in their teens, I feel that the age of sexual consent should not be above 18, and perhaps as low as 16. In this age of greater sexual freedom, I cannot imagine that most young people wait until they are 21 for their first sexual encounter. Why, then, classify them as "criminals" by holding to 21 as the age of sexual consent?

WHAT ABOUT THE MILITARY? While Great Britain's Wolfenden Committee was laboring to bring about the law which eventually passed, the military hierarchy insisted on exemptions for those in the armed services. Their demands were met with the result that homosexual acts among the military still are punishable and men so convicted may be discharged.

This also is true of the United States armed forces. It is against regulations for anyone who knows he is homosexual to be inducted. At the time of examination, the candidate is asked whether or not he is homosexual and if he is, he is granted a deferment. This, of course, often causes a dilemma for the person involved. As previously noted, homosexual persons are not usually identifiable, either physically or by mannerisms. He actually may wish to serve if he has confidence he can handle his sexual feelings without causing problems for the service. Hundreds of thousands of men, many with strong homosexual tendencies, have served faithfully and have been honorably discharged after long periods of duty. These have included both enlisted men and officers of all ranks. Young men, however, hesitate to make a statement about homosexual feelings or activities because the information goes into official records.

Anyone who is counseling young people will occasionally be confronted with the problem of homosexuality. Every situation must be dealt with on an individual basis, but I do have certain procedures I follow if a young man talks with me about service in the armed forces. First, I try to discover how committed he may be to homosexuality. Has he considered himself a homosexual for a long time? Has he been overtly involved, and how seriously? Have there been any strong personal attachments? Does he feel that he could cope with close confinement with other men, and with the stress of battle without developing severe emotional tension which might result in his being revealed?

If he answers these questions positively, I ask him to think seriously about declaring himself. Selective Service personnel I have known seem to feel that it is better for a young man to accept deferment on the basis of homosexuality. This may be wiser than being inducted and later find-

ing the emotional strain so great that the result is a volun-
tary request for discharge. He might be caught in a sexual
act considered offensive which may result in an enforced
discharge classified as "less than honorable." However, if
no sexual offense has been committed, a homosexual serviceman has the right to an honorable discharge.

Usually, when a young man does declare himself a homosexual at an examining center, an attending psychiatrist
will question him in order to substantiate his claim. I usually have suggested also, that if a man has been under
private psychiatric care he present a letter from his psychiatrist. If he has not talked with a private psychiatrist, I
suggest that he do so before the service examination and
request some documentation from the doctor. Some counselors who are known by Selective Service officials often find
that their letters are acceptable by draft boards and by the
people at the examining centers.

Before leaving the subject of military service, I should
add that since the Sex Institute at the University of Indiana
is now preparing to release its three-year study of homosexuality, two of the researchers, Colin J. Williams and Martin
S. Weinberg, have completed a survey of homosexual military personnel who have been less than honorably discharged. In the Epilogue of their carefully documented
study, Williams and Weinberg conclude:

"Regardless of the effects of less than honorable discharge, military policy concerning homosexuals is in our
view unwise, unjust, and in essence unenforcible. Such
policies are based on sterotypes of the homosexual that research has shown to be untenable and that result in dis-

crimination against a minority. Not only is the cost of training lost when a serviceman is separated for homosexual conduct, but the expenditure of investigation and separation itself seems hardly worthwhile. The majority of homosexuals who serve do so with honor, and it seems foolish to pursue this group with the ardor that authorities exhibit. If an individual's sex life does not interfere with his service activities, it should be of no concern to military authorities. If it is of such a type that causes problems, then homosexuals should be separated but not necessarily in a way that is punitive. Punitiveness should be based on the nature of the offense without regard to the serviceman's sexual orientation. The automatic use of less than honorable discharges in the military's disposition of homosexuals is in our eyes immoral." *

WHAT ABOUT EDUCATION? In counseling homosexual young people, questions often arise which concern school relationships. Some high-schoolers—boys, in particular—may have a difficult time if they have physical qualities or mannerisms which seem feminine. Earlier I have tried to make it clear that strong feminine characteristics in men, and masculine characteristics in women do not necessarily denote homosexuality, but society as a whole thinks this is true. The majority of homosexual persons look, walk, and act no differently than heterosexual individuals. They may be admired athletes or dedicated students of science. How can we help the boy who always is being "picked on"? Not

* *Homosexuals and the Military*, Colin J. Williams and Martin S. Weinberg. New York: Harper and Row, 1971.

too much, unfortunately. The great hope is to educate the general public about sexuality, to help people learn about variants, to erase prejudice as much as possible, and to hope that people will develop tolerance toward those who do not seem to measure up to some established norm.

If the boy so harassed is not truly homosexual, or even if he is, we can try to help strengthen his self-confidence, show him that inside he is not much different from other human beings, encourage him to use his talents to the best of his ability, and, above all, tell him he must not let criticism shake him. Sympathetic counseling can help, and group counseling can be especially effective.

In seeking counseling concerning education, homosexual young people may want to talk about college. There was a time when most college administrators dismissed a student or suspended him if there was evidence of a homosexual act. However, rapid changes now are taking place. Several college presidents and deans have told me that in almost every case homosexual students are not expelled or even seriously reprimanded for homosexual acts or even for establishing a homosexual life style.

This, I presume, is in keeping with the general change in college administrators concerning their sense of responsibility for the personal, private lives of students. The involvement of students in decision-making, the wide use of the "pill" and other contraceptives, the growing disappearance of single-sex dormitories, and the freedom college students are demanding and winning in so many areas of their lives are making sexual freedom a reality on our campuses. Such a spirit breeds a toleration by both students and faculty, with the result that homosexual students also have acquired rights and privileges.

Student homophile groups, recognized in most instances by the college administration, have established themselves and flourish with a considerable amount of openness and publicity. They print newspapers, hold "gay" dances, win representation on student governing bodies, and initiate social action programs. It would seem to me, then, that a college or university with a more liberal, permissive atmosphere would provide a more comfortable setting for the homosexual student than one of the more conservative educational institutions.

WHAT ABOUT VOCATION? The public has many preconceived ideas about how homosexual men and women earn a living, and high on the list is the fashion world. Many articles have been written charging homosexual designers with exerting undue influence on fashion. This is a point to be argued, but what probably is true is that many fashion designers and others working in associated areas may be homosexual persons. Hair-styling seems to attract homosexual men, particularly those with feminine characteristics, and the beauty salons seem to provide a comfortable, accepting environment for them. All of the arts seem to attract homosexual persons—theater, music, ballet, and many of the other creative disciplines. Throughout the years there has been a freedom, a tolerant "live and let live" spirit in the arts so that the expression of homosexual feelings seldom seems shocking.

However, we must not think that homosexual persons are

unusually artistic and creative (there is no real proof for such a belief) and that it is only through such work that they earn a living or reach satisfactory vocational goals. Homosexuals can and do fit into every profession and vocation. They are teachers, social workers, doctors, shopkeepers, factory employees, radio announcers, garage mechanics, and this list could be expanded to cover the entire range of vocations.

I have found that many homosexual young people are indecisive about a vocation and ask "Where will I fit best?" There is no pat answer. I send these young people to a professional vocational counselor, particularly one who understands homosexual persons, with the suggestion that a battery of tests be taken and evaluated by the counselor. I also explain that there are certain environments in which the homosexual person can live more openly and freely; however, this cannot be the determining factor if he lacks a certain talent or has other abilities and motivations.

Although it is to be hoped that social attiudes toward homosexuality will radically change within the next decade or so, it is too early for students to begin their first interview with the admissions staff of most medical, law, or social work schools (just to mention a few) with the statement, "I am a homosexual." Surely men who apply to religious seminaries or girls who plan a teaching career would have to hide their homosexual tendencies. At this time, known homosexuals cannot be employed in any government positions; a man cannot even be a postman, nor can homosexuals of either sex usually hold Civil Service jobs. Of course, there now are forces at work to challenge the constitutionality of such discrimination on the basis of whether or not the civil rights of a minority are being denied.

Painful though it is, the counselor advising the young homosexual person may have to say: "Aim for whatever life goal to which you feel called; if it is one that will allow you to express freely and honestly the sexual identity you think is yours, then this is fine; however, if your motivations move you in a direction where you cannot let your homosexuality be known, then you face the problem that millions of homosexual men and women have had to bear throughout the ages. Try to attain every possible vocational success but be careful, be discreet, be judicious about the identification of and acting out of your sexual life."

WHAT ABOUT TRANSVESTISM? This word refers to cross-dressing: the man who from time to time has a compelling desire to wear feminine clothing, or the woman who likes male attire. True transvestites, according to a national association of such persons, are not homosexual but heterosexual. To pursue this, a distinction must be made between the words "sex" and "gender." The transvestite possesses a specific sexual identity, that is, either male or female with all of the usual physical atributes, but also likes being a part of the gender of the opposite sex.

In our society, men have a difficult time expressing themselves in this regard, but women have been able to function quite well since they are able to wear blue jeans, leather belts and coats, masculine-looking footwear, men's shirts, and short hair. On the other hand, a man can scarcely appear in nylons, high heels, and a stylish silk dress. Ordinarily the only way he can do this is in his home, among a small circle of like-minded friends, or appearing in public with the hope "passing" as a woman.

Male transvestites usually are married and often their wives understand their proclivities and tolerate their cross-dressing. These men are found in all professions and vocations and they generally are successful in earning a living and maintaining their homes. Many are responsible men, love their wives, are good fathers, and make useful contributions to their churches and their communities. In their cross-dressing they are not trying to establish sexual relationships with other persons; they merely want to "act out" this particular emotional potential. Generally, trying to change such proclivities through psychiatry or other counseling is not very successful.

Although most transvestites are heterosexual, there are homosexual persons, particularly men, who appear in what is known as "drag." These, again, are men who have a desire to wear make-up and wigs, dress in feminine clothing and appear as women. These men differ considerably from heterosexual transvestites. First of all, they don't want people to believe that they really are female; they are eager to maintain their masculine identity. When they dress, they often wear rolled-up dungarees under their dresses rather than the full clothing of the female, as other transvestites do. They still are interested in sexual relationships with other men and may hope that their dressing will attract another homosexual man. They usually dress for a specific occasion—a "drag ball" or a masquerade—whereas the heterosexual transvestite dresses with some regularity, just for the sake of dressing, and when appearing in public hopes his deception will not be noticed. Heterosexual transvestites will try to walk and to talk like women, and exhibit feminine mannerisms.

WHAT ABOUT TRANSSEXUALISM? Christine Jorgensen is well-known throughout the world. She was born George Jorgensen, reared as a male, and served honorably in the United States armed forces. After beginning a career as a Hollywood photographer, he became convinced that he was a female, even though he possessed a body identifiable as male. After considerable psychotherapy, he decided to go to Denmark where for two years he was under the care of responsible, skilled doctors. He received psychological and hormonal treatment which led up to sex-change surgery involving the removal of the male genitalia and the creation of a vaginal opening. As Christine Jorgensen, she did not begin to cross-dress until the first operation had been performed. According to her autobiography, she was astounded by the reception she received upon her return to America. She never had anticipated that she would provoke so much interest and curiosity, and that she would become a celebrity almost overnight.

Christine Jorgensen is a transsexual. Such persons should not be thought of as homosexual. Although in her years as a man, Christine's sexual contacts (apparently minimal) were with other men, her desire was for the "female role." In other words, although the transsexual, before the operation, performs sexually with a person of the same sex, he or she does so as if belonging to the opposite sex. This is not being homosexual. The homosexual person wants a relationship with a person of the same sex and maintains his own same-sex identity.

I don't believe we know how many true transsexuals there are, but there are many more than once thought. A few years ago Johns Hopkins University Hospital in Baltimore opened a sexual identity clinic and followed it with sex-change surgery. Since then several other reputable hospitals in the United States have done the same. Also, many transsexuals are going to foreign cities for surgery. More and more research is being done in this area. The Erickson Foundation in Baton Rouge, Louisiana, with offices in New York, is promoting educational projects as well as assisting in some individual counseling.

Any counselor working with homosexual persons needs to be familiar with the subject of transsexualism because so-called homosexuals occasionally appear for help when actually they may be transsexual. There are real frustrations in this area for everyone involved. Knowledgeable, highly-specialized doctors are not readily available; clinics usually are not geared to cope with such cases; surgeons and hospitals often are not prepared to take on such patients and, certainly, one of the most serious problems is finances. Psychological counseling, hormonal treatment, surgery, and hospitalization, plus follow-up care make the total cost almost prohibitive for the average person. I have worked with some cases where there has not been enough money for major expenses and so a compromise is made. This is not totally satisfactory, of course, but the patient has been allowed to assume the feminine role, have his Social Security identity altered, find work as a woman, and hope that final transformation through surgery eventually will be possible.

WHAT ABOUT THE HOMOPHILE MOVEMENT? No book dealing with homosexuality would be complete without some comment on the homophile movement. The word "homophile" combines two Greek words, "homo" meaning "same" and "philos," meaning "love." One reason that this word might have been chosen was the hope that it did not have the onus the word "homosexual" seems to have. The movement began twenty years ago when organizations such as the Mattachine Society, "One" in Los Angeles, and the Daughters of Bilitis, a group of Lesbians (female homosexuals) came into being. Later other groups emerged, such as the Society of Individual Rights in San Francisco, and various locally organized groups in cities throughout the United States.

In the early years these groups were discreet, even secretive. Providing some opportunity for socialization, education for members, and counseling seemed to be their basic purpose. Then magazines and newspapers appeared, followed by efforts to educate the public through open forums and the general news media. Many organizations formed, flourished for a while, then disappeared, with others taking their places. Some groups tried to set up chapters in various cities, but with a few exceptions, the effort to create a national homophile organization has not been successful. Since 1966 there has been an annual national conference with representatives from various groups attending, but the conferences often have been marked by sharp divisions of opinion and purpose so that efforts on the national level have not gained significant strength. Occasional regional conferences attempt to keep communications open among groups. The student homophile movement has been growing on college and university campuses but, currently, these remain separate from off-campus, adult groups.

Within the past three years, the fast-developing Gay Liberation movement has come into being and, although not organized nationally, has been influential in the establishment of several organizations representing various shades of social action and militancy. New York City alone has a half-dozen or more such groups.

The Gay Liberation movement, primarily supported by young people, has brought a militancy to the homophile movement. Young people today feel that they are not willing to wait, as have generations of homosexual men and women before them, for society to make its quiet changes. These leaders believe in coercion, in confronting "the establishment," in challenging the church, educational institutions, and the government itself. They are marching with banners, protesting, taking over podiums, circulating petitions, insisting on police cooperation and protection, and wearing buttons, such as "Gay is Good!"

At the beginning they attempted to align themselves with other minorities fighting for liberties and civil rights, such as the black movement and Women's Liberation. Now there is a tendency to let their cause stand on its own feet. Their grievances are many, they are not willing to "wear masks" any longer, and they insist not only that they be heard but also that our social structures and institutions change and change fast in order that they be granted their own inalienable right to freedom and the pursuit of happiness. This movement is just beginning. It will grow, it will be noisy, and it will not quiet down until the change it demands comes into being.

6. What About a Moral Code?

How should a homosexual person act if he is a Christian? Perhaps we should first ask whether or not a homosexual can be a Christian. Heterosexual persons wonder whether homosexuals can ever inherit the Kingdom of Heaven.

Although through the ages there have been tolerant, accepting persons, my previous chapters indicate that the law, the church, the military, the educators, in fact, by far the greatest segment of society has had repressive, condemnatory attitudes about homosexuality. Not until this century, and really only within the past generation or so, has some understanding and acceptance been created as the result of the work of sociologists, anthropologists, psychologists and other researchers in the physical and social sciences. Certain sociological factors also have begun to remove the fear of homosexuality. Among these may very well be the realization that overpopulation is perhaps one of the most serious threats the world now faces. Couples are being asked to give serious consideration to limiting the number of children they have, and young people now feel that it would be wrong to have more than two children. I have heard social scientists state—and seriously—that homosexuality at least helps control the population.

So many myths about homosexuality have frightened people that they often feel a homosexual person is so reprehensible that he has no right to the privileges of the church. Foremost among these myths is the belief that homosexuals, particularly men, are molesters of children. This fear is implanted in our minds when we are so young that it is most difficult to dispel it. Facts, of course, do not bear out such a fear. The truth seems to be that the homosexual man actually is less apt to be sexually involved with a child than the heterosexual male.

In Study Guild Number 11, *Sexual Encounters Between Adults and Children*, published by the Sex Information and Educational Council of the United States, there is this statement:

"The man who is sexually interested in children is rarely a homosexual with well-developed interests in adult males, and he is seldom a member of the 'gay' community. Thus, police work that directs itself to such populations when an offense has been committed is misdirected. More often, the offender is a single or married male who lives a relatively conventional life with only sporadic, or no adult homosexual contact. In many cases, here too the offense arises from some stress that occurs in the man's life. When violence occurs, the offender usually has another major behavior disorder, such as alcoholism, and may have a history of nonsexual criminality."

All those who work to help people with sexual problems are in almost total agreement that a distinction must be made between the child-molester and the homosexual person. It is true that there are occasional instances where a homosexual person has been involved sexually with a child. But this is rare, considering the number of homosexual persons in the general population and the incidence of homosexual physical acts.

It must be made clear that, from the sexual point of view, the homosexual is interested in emotional and physical involvement with a person of the same sex who is mature interesting and exciting—just as the heterosexual would seek someone of the opposite sex who was interesting and exciting. The average heterosexual man or woman is not basically motivated to seek sex with a child; neither is the homosexual person.

I repeat my question, "How should a homosexual person act if he is a Christian?" There are those who wonder whether such a person had any right to be Christian. In spite of those who still consider a homosexual physical act to be abominable, almost unpardonable, there are theologians, church leaders, and lay Christians who accept the homosexual person as both a Christian and a churchman. There remain, however, questions as to how the homosexual person is to be allowed to function in terms of the established Christian ethic.

I must ask again, as I did in the first chapter, just what the Christian sexual ethic really is in today's world. I see no consensus on this point. First, what has been through the centuries the established, generally accepted Judeo-Christian sexual ethic? Briefly stated, is it not that no man or woman will have any genital contact with another person until marriage has taken place? Until recently, even masturbation was considered sinful. Such an ethic has insisted further that should one partner in the marriage become physically or emotionally ill so that no physical relationship is possible, or if both are separated for long periods of time, possibly many years, still neither involved in the marriage may experience physical sex.

I cannot help wondering how completely or how consistently this ethic has been or is being adhered to. There have been and there are many, of course, who have fulfilled the letter of the law in this regard. What this percentage is, in proportion to the total population, I do not know, but I suspect that it is not as high as the established church has hoped it to be.

Sexual revolution or not, we must face reality. During the past few years, attitudes and practices have developed among men and women of all ages which simply do not fit this long-established Judeo-Christian sexual ethic. For good or for ill man is seeing and accepting himself as an emotional, sexual person. More than this, he is trying to deal with his sexuality in what he feels to be a far more honest, open way than those before him. He not only is challenging the sexual dictates of the past but he is doing so with the belief that he should neither be cut off from faith in Jesus Christ nor denied the rights and privileges of his church.

To pursue this further, let us look at the social-sexual changes taking place:

(1) The institution of marriage, as it has been known, is

greatly threatened. Statistics differ, but indicate that one out of four or one out of three marriages now end in divorce. Marriages between young people under 21 are a real statistical risk, with some states reporting that more than half fail. Multiple marriages, once prevalent only in Hollywood, are now widespread.

(2) The idea that the primary purpose of sex is the procreation of children is challenged. Fear of overpopulation is partly responsible; so are economic pressures which are pushing couples toward a higher standard of family living and beyond-high-school education for their children. But even more important are the new concepts about the meaning of both sex and marriage which have come to the forefront.

(3) Contraceptives, particularly "the pill," are easily available. In some countries they may be bought from dispensing machines on the street.

(4) Fear of veneral diseases has been reduced. Although a serious national health problem, still the public believes that through modern medicine veneral disease is now more easily treated and controlled. Public health offices provide free, confidential cure and care.

(5) Several organizations such as Planned Parenthood, which once dealt only with married persons, now advise and assist single women and girls.

(6) Many college and university administrations have abdicated the responsibility they once felt they should exert over the personal lives of students, male and female. These changes are increasing fast. In 1967, women's dormitories at a large southern university literally held "bed checks"

each night; now women are allowed to stay out all night if they wish.

(7) The mobility and freedom of today's young people, both men and women, to pack a knapsack and go off to see America or to see the world gives them opportunity for sexual expression which previous generations did not have.

(8) The automobile always has been considered by social scientists as contributing considerably to greater sexual license. Now, of course, the number of cars owned by young people has increased manyfold.

(9) *Playboy Magazine* has been a huge financial success. It is extensively read by young people. Its philosophy of sexual freedom is widely accepted. This is just one of many magazines, books, and other publications which emphasize sex.

(10) The movies, television, theater, the visual arts, even the dance have themes based on all varieties of sexual experience. Efforts to establish a movie rating scale have not kept young people from seeing practically whatever they want to see.

(11) Articles and reports published by scholars, particularly social scientists, which subscribe to a freer sexual code, plus research by the Sex Institute at the University of Indiana, SIECUS, the National Institute of Mental Health, and Masters and Johnson all come to the attention of young people.

(12) The increasing availability of abortions in this country and abroad because of relaxation of laws has reduced the fear of pregnancy.

(13) The breakdown of authority is a significant element.

The law itself, as we have noted, is undergoing serious change; parental authority is not very effective, and the church's demands are being challenged. These are among the forces which, pressing upon youth today, make them question how plausible the tightly circumscribed Judeo-Christian ethic really is.

What sexual decisions can we honestly expect today's young people to make? Is the traditional Judeo-Christian ethic the only one we can hold up or must we offer some alternative? Obviously, there still are strong arguments for preaching and teaching what long has been the accepted code. Many churches insist on holding fast to strict Christian morality. This, of course, is and must be their privilege. Even in the midst of today's sexual freedom, there are young people who also hold firm to such precepts. They deserve respect and are to be commended for standing up for what they believe, for practicing what they preach. But every Christian young person may not feel bound by a moral theology which maintains that sexual behavior is to be limited to certain relationships. Are there not some Christian principles we can apply to personal relationships which involve sexuality? I believe there are.

(1) What about the other person with whom we are sexually involved? Is this person being hurt, misled, or compromised in any way? Are we taking advantage, being selfish or using coercion—not merely physical but emotional?

(2) In a heterosexual relationship, what about pregnancy? What kind of moral responsibility are we prepared to take, should that take place?

(3) What kind of pledges or commitments are involved in the relationship? Are they being made casually, without any real intention on our part?

(4) Are our physical relationships a real part of our total emotional life, or are they merely for physical outlet and gratification?

(5) How should we react sexually with someone we know has commitments they know should be honored?

(6) Do we accept the position that genital acts have nothing whatsoever to do with our moral conduct, or do we think of genital sex as being "sacramental"?

Once again I return to the question, "How should the homosexual person act as a Christian?" If we accept the fact that he or she has the right to a full sexuality, then the points just made (excepting, of course, that of pregnancy) may apply.

I am saying, in other words, that I see no reason why the same Christian sexual ethic should not be applicable to both heterosexual and homosexual persons. As should be apparent from this text, the only real difference between heterosexuality and homosexuality is the choice of sex object. There will be some readers who feel that homosexual genital acts must be thought of differently because they are not regarded as natural. This is an old argument which to my mind is not honestly tenable. I quite realize that there are Christian theologians who depend heavily on the un-naturalness of homosexual acts. To them the only natural sex act is coitus. However, Masters and Johnsons, as well as other competent researchers in the study of human sexuality and marriage, report that sexual contacts between men and women are so varied as to include mouth-genital (both cunnilingus and fellatio) as well as anal intercourse.

With homosexual persons, studies indicate the most prevalent practice is mutual masturbation, with fellatio second, and anal intercourse last—and practiced by a limited number of persons. There are those researchers who say that the only unnatural genital act is that which is impossible to perform.

How do we determine what is natural and what is unnatural? For instance, is it natural for a baby to nurse from a bottle? Or for a man to shave? Or for people who live in very hot climates to wear clothes? Perhaps it is not natural for man to cook his food, to eat lobsters, or to fly in airplanes. For some men it is natural to desire sexual contact with a woman; other men find sexual fulfillment with someone of their own sex.

Where there are questions about how homosexual persons can meet the requirements of the Christian sexual code, it is important to realize that the majority of homosexual persons manage their daily lives in much the same way as heterosexual persons—they work and earn, maintain apartments and homes, pay their taxes and their bills, shop, are involved in politics or community projects, have vacations, go to church. There is, of course, talk about a "homosexual way of life," a "homosexual subculture." This involves a minority of homosexual persons, but some comments about it should be made.

I do not know exactly what a "homosexual life-style" is, but I presume it could refer to homosexual men and women who usually congregate in the larger cities because they feel less lonely, meet others with similar interests, discover a more exciting life, and have some assurance of a kind of anonymity if they want it. The "Gay bar" has become the rendezvous for many of them—a place to meet friends, to make new acquaintances, to find sexual contacts. Particularly, it also is a place where one would feel less lonely, less left out. Unfortunately, the bar does not always accomplish what is expected. It is cliquish, can be hard and cruel, and a person may leave far lonelier than he was when he entered. In large cities such as New York and San Francisco there are bars for all types of people: the sophisticated, the artistic, the collegiate, the conservative, the promiscuous, and so on.

Homosexual persons often find it difficult to locate each other. Some get involved in seeking others in known "cruising areas"—particular streets and parks, or perhaps, department stores. They make contacts which usually are only for sex—the kind often referred to as "the one night stand." Cruising is not without problems because many "hustlers" (those wanting money in return for sex) are heterosexuals who may try to blackmail their partners or even harm them. Such sex also makes one especially vulnerable to venereal disease.

Homosexuals have been severely criticized because of this bar-and-street life; however, with some bitterness, they retort that they have been shunted aside by society into a "shadowy existence."

No book dealing with homosexuality would be objective if it did not emphasize the anguish, anxiety, pain, even despair that too often are part of a homosexual's life style. For the average heterosexual person, life is none too easy in our fast-moving, complex, and demanding society; the path traveled by homosexual men and women is just that much more rocky, more tortuous.

Twenty years ago, an author identifying himself as homosexual and writing under the pseudonym of Donald Webster Cory, published a book, *The Homosexual in America* (New York: Castle Books, 1951). In it he expressed not only his own feelings and thoughts but also those of many others who shared his situation. He wrote:

"We homosexuals are a minority, but more than that, an intensified minority, with all the problems that arise from being a separate group facing us that are faced by other groups, and with a variety of important problems that are unshared by most minorities. The ethnic groups can take refuge in the comfort and pride of their own, in the warmth of family and friends, in the acceptance of themselves among the most enlightened people around them. But not the homosexuals. Those closest to us, whose love we are in extreme need of, accept us for what we are not. Constantly and unceasingly we carry a mask, and without interruption we stand on guard lest our secret, which is our very essence, be betrayed. . . .

"Society has handed me a mask to wear, a ukase that it shall never be lifted except in the presence of those who hide with me behind its protective shadows. Everywhere I go at all times and before all sections of society, I pretend. As my being rebels against the hypocrisy that is forced upon me, I realize that its greatest repercussion has been the wave of self-doubt that I must harbor. Because I am unable to stand up before the world and acknowledge that I am what I am, because I carry around with me a fear and a shame I find that I endanger my confidence in myself and in my way of living, and that this confidence is required for the enjoyment of life."

Now that a whole new generation has filled the gap between the writing of these words and the present day, it is to be hoped that homosexual persons can live more comfortably today. However, in all honesty, the fact must be faced that progress toward acceptance has been slow, and those who would express their homosexuality may well be faced with the same social restrictions, the same rejection, and know even the same anger that shows through in the words quoted above.

It is true that our social institutions, including the church, have not wanted to recognize the homosexual person as an admitted homosexual, or to accept his efforts to establish his own personal relationships. However, a few breakthroughs are taking place. For instance, some local churches have helped organize social groups for homosexuals, giving them permission to meet in parish houses and to hold special worship services.

Many homosexual persons are as committed to a Christian moral code as are heterosexual men and women. References often are made to the fact that homosexual men and women rarely establish long-term relationships. Most people believe that homosexual friendships are short-lived, without firm roots; they are thought to be marked with infidelity, bickering, pettiness, shallowness. We must admit that many attempts to establish long-term relationships are thwarted, are blighted too soon. At the same time, through the years many social forces have combined to destroy such liaisons and few helps have been created to support their maintenance. Just the opposite is true of heterosexual relationships.

It is my opinion that counseling through many channels should be made as available to homosexual couples as to married heterosexual couples. In spite of all the pressures, many homosexual relationships not only survive but also have the same qualities inherent in a good heterosexual marriage. Counselors who work in this area know of homosexual relationships which have lasted many years.

There are those who believe that if homosexual couples seriously wish to live responsible, moral lives, then there should be a commitment comparable to marriage. There are homosexual couples, both men and women, who do feel this way. Some have had their relationship blessed by a minister, have exchanged rings, and have made pledges similar to those of the established marriage services. Some homosexual couples seek legalization of such contracts by civil authorities so that they may jointly own property, inherit from one another, and acquire certain tax equities.

Countering this position are other homosexual couples who wonder why they should try to pattern their lives after Christian marriage which they claim shows serious signs of deterioration in today's society, rather than great strength.

What, then, about a Christian moral code for the Christian homosexual person? Should he not expect to live according to the same moral code as other Christians? Should he not meet the same sexual ethic as well—except for the responsibility for pregnancy and other differences which separate the homosexual relationship from the established marriage bond?

Beyond that, if he is a Christian, the other rules should apply. Does not this imply, then, that he deserves the acceptance, the respect, the concern of other Christians? Should he not have all the rights and privileges that he was granted at his baptism, to be a "member of Christ, the child of God, and an inheritor of the kingdom of heaven"?

Epilogue

Charles Dickens begins his *Tale of Two Cities* with these words: "It was the best of times, it was the worst of times." And so . . . what of young people today? Is this the "best" or the "worst" of times? I say this is the "best."

How do I dare say this when we are faced with continuing war in the Far East, with a frightening drug culture, and with a decreasing commitment to Christianity coupled with deepening distrust of the institutional church?

Still, I reply "best", because I firmly believe that young people today have the opportunity for a freedom which earlier generations never knew.

The founding fathers of this nation used the phrase "created free and equal." But long before, Jesus of Nazareth had declared, "Ye shall know the truth and the truth shall make you free" (John 8:32). Freedom has been talked about for centuries; now its chance of becoming more of a reality is greater than ever before. Many barriers—racial, religious, ideological, sexual—which separated man from man for so long seem to be crumbling; even the chasm between the roles of male and female is closing and the new word "unisex" is no longer novelty but fact.

In the Foreword the words "youth" and "core of faith" are used together and I truly believe they belong together. Youth can have a new faith in freedom for all men; yet it need not abandon its faith in the principles upon which this nation was founded nor on the Gospel of Christ. With faith in the knowledge that God created all men to be free, today's young people will see more and more barriers fall. Because they have a *desire* to understand and to accept, which those before them did not have, they *will* know and accept, not only their own feelings but those of others as well.

And so in "the best of times" the homosexual person may find the world a better place in which to live. Today's young people may provide this freedom, this equality which, long guaranteed, now grows closer to reality.

A Selected Bibliography

Bailey, Derrick Sherwin. *Homosexuality and the Western Christian Tradition*. London: Longmans, Green and Co., 1955.

Becker, Raymond de. *The Other Face of Love*. Translation by Margaret Crosland and Alan Daventry. New York: Grove Press, 1969.

Benjamin, Harry. *The Transsexual Phenomenon*. New York: The Julian Press, Inc., 1966.

Benson, R. O. D. *In Defense of Homosexuality*. New York: The Julian Press, 1965.

Bieber, Irving. *Homosexuality: A Psychoanalytic Study of Male Homosexuals*. New York: Basic Books, 1962.

Cappon, Daniel. *Toward an Understanding of Homosexuality*. Englewood Cliffs, New Jersey: Prentice Hall, Inc., 1965.

Churchill, Wainwright. *Homosexual Behavior Among Males*. New York: Hawthorn Books, Inc., 1967.

Cory, Donald Webster. *The Homosexual in America*. New York: Castle, 1960.

Cory, Donald Webster. *The Lesbian in America*. New York: Citadel Press, 1964.

Eglinton, J. Z. *Greek Love*. New York: Oliver Layton Press, 1964.

Ellis, Albert, Dr., *Homosexuality: Its Causes and Cure*. New York: Lyle Stewart, Inc., 1965.

Ford, Clellan S. and Beach, Frank A., Ph.D. *Patterns of Sexual Behavior*. New York: Harper, 1951.

Gross, Alfred A., Dr. *Strangers in Our Midst*. Washington: Public Affairs Press, 1962.

Gross, Alfred A., Dr. *A Primer of Ethics*. Sandy, Oregon: St. Paul's Press, 1971.

Hatterer, Lawrence J. *Changing Homosexuality in the Male: Treatment for Men Troubled by Homosexuality*. New York: McGraw Hill, 1970.

Hauser, Richard. *The Homosexual Society*. London: The Bodley Head, 1962.

Henry, George W. *Sex Variants: A Study of Homosexual Patterns*. New York: Hoeber, 1948.

Heron, Alastair (ed.). *Towards a Quaker View of Sex*. London: Friends Home Service Committee, 1963. Revised edition, 1964.

Hoffman, Martin. *The Gay World*. New York–London: Basic Books, Inc., 1968.

Hooker, Evelyn. *The Homosexual Community*. In Proc. XIVth int. Congr. appl. Psychol, Personality Research. Vol 2. Copenhagen: Munksgaard, 1962.

Hooker, Evelyn. *Male Homosexuality*. In N. L. Farberow (Ed.) Taboo Topics. New York: Atherton, 1963.

Humphreys. Laud. *Tearoom Trade*. Chicago: Aldine Publishing Co., 1970.

Jones, H. Kimball. *Toward a Christian Understanding of the Homosexual*. New York: Association Press, 1966.

Kinsey, A. C., Pomeroy, W. B. and Martin, C. E. *Sexual Behavior in the Human Male*, London and Philadelphia: Saunders, 1948.

Krich, A. M. *The Homosexuals*. (*As Seen by Themselves and Thirty Authorities*). New York: The Citadel Press, 1961.

Magee, Bryan. *One in Twenty*. New York: Stein and Day, 1966.

Marmor, Judd, Editor. *Sexual Inversion*. New York: Basic Books, Inc., 1965.

Oberholtzer, W. Dwight. *Is Gay Good?* Philadelphia: The
    Westminster Press, 1971.
Pittinger, Norman. *Time for Consent?* London: SCM Press,
    Ltd., 1967.
Ruitenbeek, Hendrik M. (Ed.) *The Problem of Homosexuality
    in Modern Society.* E. P. Dutton and Company, Inc.,
    1963.
Schofield, Michael. *Sociological Aspects of Homosexuality.*
    Boston: Little, Brown and Company, 1965.
Schofield, Michael. *Society and the Homosexual.* New York:
    E. P. Dutton and Company, Inc., 1953.
Schur, Edwin M. *Crimes Without Victims.* Englewood Cliffs,
    New Jersey: Prentice Hall, Inc., 1965.
Socarides, Charles W. *The Overt Homosexual.* New York–Lon-
    don: Grune and Stratton, 1968.
Stearn, Jess. *The Sixth Man.* Garden City, New York: Double-
    day and Company, Inc., 1961.
Ullerstam, Lars. *The Erotic Minorities.* New York: Grove
    Press, Inc., 1966.
Weltge, Ralph W. (ed.). *The Same Sex: An Appraisal of
    Homosexuality.* Philadelphia: Pilgrim Press, 1969.
West, Donald J. *Homosexuality.* Chicago: Aldine Publishing
    Company, 1967.
Willis, Stanley E. II, M.D. *Understanding and Counseling the
    Male Homosexual.* Boston: Little, Brown, 1967.
The Wolfenden Report. New York: Stein and Day, Inc., 1963.
Wood, Robert W. *Christ and the Homosexual.* New York–
    Washington–Hollywood: Vantage Press, Inc., 1960.